# THE BLITZ

## Fiona Reynoldson

# THE HOME FRONT

THE BLITZ
EVACUATION
PRISONERS OF WAR
PROPAGANDA
RATIONING
WOMEN'S WAR

Editor: Catherine Ellis
Series designer: Nick Cannan
Consultant: Terry Charman, researcher and historian at the Imperial War Museum

First published in 1990 by
Wayland (Publishers) Limited
61 Western Road, Hove
East Sussex BN3 1JD

**British Library Cataloguing in Publication Data**
Reynoldson, Fiona
The blitz.
I. England. Air raids by Germany. Luftwaffe, 1939–1944
I. Title  II. Series
940.54212

ISBN 1–85210–874–6

Typeset by Rachel Gibbs, Wayland
Printed and bound by MacLehose & Partners Ltd., Portsmouth

# CONTENTS

The Early Days of War **4**

Air Raid Precautions **6**

The Black-out **8**

7 September 1940 **10**

London in the Blitz **12**

Underground Shelters **14**

Damage in the Blitz **16**

Public Shelters **18**

The Raid on Coventry **20**

All over Britain **22**

The Fire of London **24**

Fires and Devastation **26**

The Last Months of War **28**

Glossary **30**

Projects **30**

Books to Read **31**

Index **32**

# The Early days of War

*A German advertisement showing Stukas about to dive-bomb enemy ships. The Nazis used Stukas in their lightning attacks (blitzkrieg) on countries.*

The Second World War started in September 1939. Nothing much happened for a few months. Then in the spring of 1940, Germany defeated France and drove the British Army back to Dunkirk. Suddenly the German Army was only just across the Channel.

'Men of the undefeated British Expeditionary Force have been coming home from France.' (BBC newsreader, 31 May 1940.)

This sounded like a hopeful announcement. Nearly a quarter of a million British soldiers had been brought back to Britain by boat from Dunkirk. In fact, they were exhausted, dirty and defeated. They had left all their guns, tanks and lorries in France.

The French and the British had given the Nazis little trouble. Now Hitler wanted to knock Britain out of the war. He called his plan Operation Sealion – this was the invasion of Britain. The British knew the situation was serious.

*Hitler called his plan to invade Britain Operation Sealion. It was never carried out.*

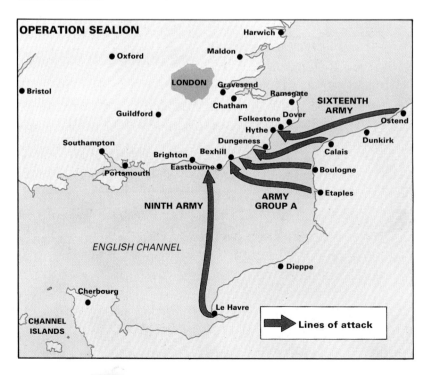

# THE BLITZ

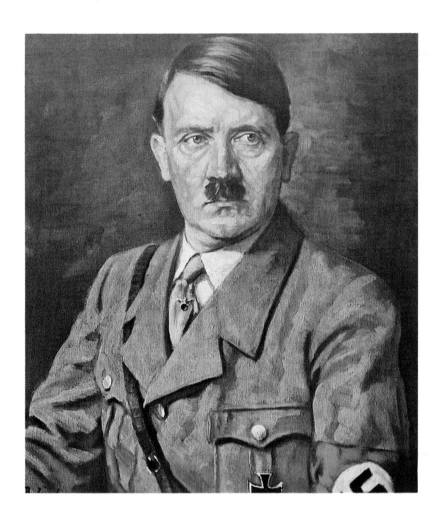

'We shall defend our island whatever the cost may be. We shall fight on the beaches, we shall fight on the landing grounds, we shall fight in the fields and in the streets, we shall fight in the hills, we shall never surrender.' (Winston Churchill, 1940.)

Before the Nazis could invade Britain they had to destroy the Royal Air Force (RAF), otherwise British aeroplanes would bomb the German Army as it sailed to Britain. So the Battle of Britain started. All through the long, hot summer days the British and Germans fought in the skies over Britain. This battle was vital. By early September, the British expected to be invaded any day.

Both sides lost many aeroplanes and pilots, but the Royal Air Force was not destroyed. Hitler had to change his tactics. Perhaps he could force the British to surrender by terrifying London.

# Air Raid Precautions

People had expected bombing for years. The government thought that 100,000 tonnes of bombs would fall on London in the first fortnight of war. Thousands of people would be killed and injured. Hospitals were cleared ready for the bomb victims. Millions of cardboard coffins were made. Lime pits were dug for mass burials.

Gas had been used against troops in the First World War. The government assumed it would be used again, but that this time gas would be dropped on ordinary people. It gave out over forty million gas masks to protect people.

'Young children had blue and red ones that looked like Mickey Mouse. Soldiers had very grand ones with round eyepieces and a trunk like an elephant. Ours had a short trunk and a large window for our eyes. The moment you put it on the window misted up, blinding you.' (*Children of the Blitz*, Robert Westall.)

*Cigarette cards, showing the respirator, or gas mask.*

Left *Many people worked to fill sacks with sand. These sandbags were piled up to protect buildings, particularly the windows.*

Below *Steel air raid shelters being delivered to families in London in 1938. People had to erect them themselves.*

In fact, gas was not used, and people soon gave up carrying their gas masks.

Air Raid Precautions (ARP) began in 1938. Some people erected shelters in their gardens. Public shelters were built. Air raid wardens were called for.

'I joined the Warden's Service because it seemed to me to be the most active and obviously helpful Civil Defence occupation open to women . . .

'I was given a tin hat, a whistle and a CD respirator [gas mask]. The Post Warden took me on a tour of the seventeen public shelters in our area. I worked out that the wardens kept the paraffin lamps in shelters alight and held the keys.' (*Raiders Overhead*, Barbara Nixon.)

Some people came up with funny ideas for protection against bombing:

'Why not a light metal umbrella, proof against shrapnel? It would offer more protection, over a wider area than a steel helmet.' (A letter in *Picture Post*, 19 October 1940.)

# The Black-out

Full-time wardens earned £3.00 a week. At the beginning of the war nothing happened. No bombs, no gas, no invasion. People grumbled that the wardens were paid for sitting in their posts and playing cards. Some said ARP stood for ''Anging Round Pubs''!

However, the wardens did enforce the black-out. Everyone was afraid that if German bombers could see the lights of houses they would know they were over a town and would drop their bombs. For the first weeks of the war the black-out was total:

'All windows, doors, skylights or openings which would show a light must be screened so that no light can be seen from outside. Do not use a light in a room unless the blind or curtain is drawn, and remember that a light at the back of a house is just as visible from the air as one at the front.' (*Air Raid Precautions 1939.*)

People had to buy thick, dark curtains. Some people stuck brown paper on their windows. In some big factories all the windows were painted black, and workers inside had the lights on all day.

All the street lights were turned off. Headlights on cars were banned. Traffic lights were blacked out except

*White stripes were painted on pavement kerbs and lampposts to make them more visible during the black-out. This cow is also being given white stripes. Many grazing areas were more open than they are today, and animals sometimes wandered on to the roads.*

Left and below *When the government realized how dangerous the black-out was, it put up posters to warn people to take care.*

for a tiny cross in the middle. No bombs had been dropped yet, but there were masses of road accidents! In the first few weeks 4,000 people were killed on the roads, so cars were then allowed to use hooded headlights.

Everywhere was inky black. The best answer for pedestrians was a torch, but even that had to be covered with tissue paper and shone downwards or a warden would pounce. Fines for breaking the black-out were quite heavy.

# 7 September 1940

German night raids on Britain began during the summer of 1940, while the Battle of Britain was raging in the South of England. Everyone expected an invasion any day. People watched the beaches. They watched the sea. They watched the skies.

The invasion didn't come but the Blitz did. The first big daylight raid on London was on 7 September. About 350 bombers, escorted by 650 fighters, attacked London's docks and oil refineries. In the afternoon a second raid began:

'At 4.43 p.m. the sirens wailed . . . the women were frankly fussed and ran but nobody was seriously frightened . . . Within a few minutes a large V-shaped formation of planes flew over us . . . The tiny machines glinted in the sunlight. That afternoon the danger was still remote from us. It was the East End that was

*Firemen playing hoses on burning warehouses in the Surrey Docks. Even when the stores were soaked, the heat was great enough for the fires to flare up again after the hoses were turned off.*

*One of the many fires in the East London Surrey Commercial Dock on 7 September 1940.*

"getting it". We could see the miniature planes circling round and round the target area . . . As one set of planes flew off, another in V-formation would fly in and then circle.

'Presently we saw a white cloud rising; it looked like an evening cumulus cloud, but it grew steadily . . . A fire engine went by up the main road. The cloud grew to such a size that we gasped; there could not ever in history have been so gigantic a fire. Another fire engine raced by, then a third, then a fourth, clanging their bells frenziedly as they shot across the traffic lights; nearly every fire appliance in London was heading east. As evening drew on the huge barrage balloons turned pink in the sunset light; or was it firelight?' (*Raiders Overhead.*)

The bombing lasted all through the night until dawn of 8 September. This was the beginning of the Blitz.

*A Dornier DO17 – a German medium bomber, known as the 'flying pencil'. The Junkers JU88 was the most successful German bomber.*

# London in the Blitz

The night of 7 September was called Black Saturday. 448 people were killed, and 1,600 people were badly injured. Hundreds of families lost their homes. In the East End of London people ran to shelter amid the bricks, dust, smoke and smell of the bombs.

'The most common saying by men, as well as women, was that this wasn't war, it was murder, they wouldn't stand for it. The loudest cry however, was: where were the guns?' (*Raiders Overhead.*)

It was five nights before more anti-aircraft guns were brought into London. Then they opened up with a noise that cheered up everyone.

'It was calculated that nearly 2,000 shells were fired for every aircraft destroyed.' (*A People's War*, Peter Lewis.)

*A rescue worker searching a bombed house in Dover.*

But the anti-aircraft guns, the searchlights and the barrage balloons did the job they were supposed to do.

They kept the German bombers high in the sky. This made it difficult for the bombers to hit the targets they wanted to hit.

The bombers came the next night and the next. They came for fifty-seven nights in a row. Very soon they were bombing the whole of London. This writer was in Hampstead:

'... suddenly there was the weirdest sort of scratching sound just above the roofs ... then the most God-awful crash. I felt the earth juddering under me as I sat. I remember racing towards the house and it seemed as if the whole air was falling apart, quite silently ... Suddenly I was on my face, just inside the kitchen door. ... I clutched the floor as if it was a cliff face that I had to hang on to, or else I'd fall – actually I was lying down already.' (Young observer for the Mass-Observation Archive.)

Bottom *Members of the Home Guard training with a heavy anti-aircraft gun in London.*

Below *Powerful searchlights were shone up into the sky so that bombers could be seen in the beams of light.*

# Underground Shelters

*Serving food to a family sheltering in the Underground.*

As the bombing raids continued people became tired from lack of sleep. They became nervous. But they also became more used to the bombs.

Some people went to public shelters. Others had Anderson shelters in their back gardens. Some people in London decided to use the Underground stations to shelter in. The government was afraid that people might go underground and never come up again.

'Thousands upon thousands the next evening pushed their way into Liverpool Street Station and demanded to be let down to shelter. At first the authorities wouldn't agree to it and they called out the soldiers to bar the way . . . The people would not give up. A great yell went up and the gates were opened.' (*The World is a Wedding*, Bernard Kops.)

*People not only sheltered on the platforms of the London Underground (the deepest places to shelter), but also in the passageways.*

At other stations people bought tickets and went down to the platform. They just stayed there and refused to leave. Sometimes they went along the line to the next station.

> 'I would scoot out of the train ahead of the family and under the legs of people, unravelling the three or four scarves tied round me. I bagged any space I could along the platform. The family followed.' (*The World is a Wedding*.)

About 60,000 people sheltered in 79 of London's Underground stations. The government gave up trying to stop them. People queued for places. The early days in the tubes were grim:

> 'The stench was frightful, urine and excrement mixed with strong carbolic, sweat and dirty humanity.' (*Shelter People – The War Papers* part 12.)

Gradually things improved. The Salvation Army and the Women's Voluntary Service ran shuttle services of buns and drinks from station to station. Most children adapted easily and thought it was a good game.

*A bus stuck in a crater after a direct hit on Balham Underground Station in October 1940. Many who sheltered in the Underground were killed.*

# Damage in the Blitz

Along with the night raids, daylight raids continued until early October. There were two main ideas behind the daylight raids. First, to force the RAF to attack the German bombers and be shot down by the German fighters. Second, to terrify the people in British cities so that Britain would surrender and Hitler would not have to invade Britain at all.

However, the bombing was not heavy enough to make people want to surrender. It was nowhere near as heavy as people had feared it would be.

'Last Thursday night 180 persons were killed in London as a result of 251 tons of bombs. That is to say, it took one ton of bombs to kill three quarters of a person . . . It would take ten years, at the present rate of bombing for half the houses of London to be demolished.' (Winston Churchill, 8 October 1940.)

*A building collapsing in Victoria Street, London, after a night of heavy bombing.*

HOLDING THE LINE!

*Heavy "Stirling" bombers raid the Nazi Baltic port of Lübeck and leave the docks ablaze*

BACK THEM UP!

Meanwhile, the RAF had also been bombing German cities. On the whole the effect was the same in Germany as in Britain. People were angered and frightened by the bombs but it did not make them want to surrender. They came out of their shelters or homes every morning to inspect the damage. In London, on the night of 15 October 1940:

'540 tons of high explosive caused all rail services to be stopped or cut to less than one third . . . Stations and roads were blocked by UXBs (unexploded bombs) . . . Three water mains, a reservoir, three gas works, two power stations, three dock areas and the BBC were hit and damaged by bombs. 900 fires were reported.' (*The Defence of the United Kingdom*, B. Collier.)

That was the thirty-eighth night in a row that London had been bombed.

Above left *An American poster of Winston Churchill, the prime minister. He was seen as a bulldog because he would not give up against the Germans.*

Above right *A British poster showing British bombers raiding the German Baltic port of Lübeck.*

# Public Shelters

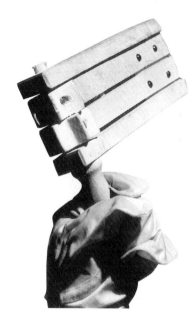

Above *A warden's rattle, used as a warning sound.*

People got used to hearing the air raid warning siren every night. It was a wailing noise. Some people called it Moaning Minnie.

'We left everything and ran down to the shelter. We sat on the wooden benches, listening . . .' (Paul McIntyre, South London.)

If you were outside you soon heard the throb of the planes' engines and the sound of the bombs dropping:

'I remember the whistle of the bombs, louder and louder as they got nearer.' (J.H. Moore, Coventry.)

Right *Many shelters flooded easily. A Shelter Marshal makes his round in inches of water.*

Other bombs sounded like the tearing of sheets. Small fire bombs clattered on roofs. The anti-aircraft guns thudded and their shrapnel rained down on the pavements. Every now and then there was a crash as a house blew up. Then came the crackle of flames.

The air raid wardens got to know everyone in their area. They knew where every family sheltered – in an Anderson shelter in the garden, in a cellar, or under the stairs (the strongest part of the house). Some stayed in their comfortable beds and refused to shelter. If a house was hit the wardens knew where to start digging to look for people.

Many people living in flats in the cities used public shelters. Wardens toured them during raids. Some people did not trust the shelters and thought they would collapse. Many shelters were badly built. There was a shortage of cement, so the bricks were hardly stuck together. Few shelters had proper toilets, and many had nothing more to sit on than wooden benches. The trouble was that no one had expected raids to last a long time. Slowly, as people began to spend all night in the shelters, improvements were made.

*The steel garden shelters were called Anderson shelters. This one has survived while the house is rubble.*

# The Raid on Coventry

By late October 1940, Germany had given up the idea of invading Britain. It seemed more important now to bomb the British towns where aeroplanes, tanks and guns were made.

On 14 November the Germans attacked Coventry. Coventry was a small, compact city compared to London. There was a bright moon that night. The German bombers came in waves all through the night. The whole centre of the city was burnt out. Lin Grove was a fireman with the Solihull Brigade:

'We were called to attend at about 5 a.m. and arrived just after the all-clear. All entries to the city were blocked, and we were engaged all day clearing debris, chipping molten glass and seeking wounded. I was near the cathedral – now a complete ruin.'

Below *The centre of Coventry, the morning after it was bombed.* Inset *Notices appeared in Coventry warning people that the water was unsafe to drink without boiling.*

CITY OF COVENTRY
PREVENTION OF TYPHOID FEVER

In view of present damage to DRAINAGE communications in the City, special precautions against Typhoid Fever are advised

BOIL ALL DRINKING WATER

WILLS'S CIGARETTES

A CHAIN OF BUCKETS

WILLS'S CIGARETTES

LIGHT TRAILER FIRE-PUMP

WILLS'S CIGARETTES

THE STIRRUP HAND PUMP

WILLS'S CIGARETTES

TWO-MEN PORTABLE MANUAL FIRE-PUMP IN ACTION

*Fire was a terrible hazard during the Blitz. These cigarette cards show different ways of dealing with a fire.*

*Churchill knew that Coventry was going to be attacked because the British had broken the German secret code. However, it was important the Germans did not know the British could understand their secret messages, so Churchill could not order the evacuation of the city.*

That night in Coventry 568 people were killed, and 863 seriously injured. Nothing was left. Shops and pubs were closed. There was no water; the drains were damaged. One of the first notices that went up at the police stations was: 'BOIL ALL DRINKING WATER'. There were no buses or trains, no telephones. No one knew what was happening. This was one of the most frightening things – the collapse of people's ordinary lives.

Other cities soon suffered German raids, but often the real object of the raid failed. In Coventry twenty-one factories were hit. Nine more were damaged so that they could not carry on working. Not for long however:

'Some of the factories were just covered in tarpaulins. The only heating would be from coke braziers. And they stuck at the machines day and night, twelve hours at a time, seven days a week.' (Jack Jones, Transport and General Workers' Union.)

# All over Britain

Above *Bombed houses were often left empty. Stealing from them was called looting and was punishable by death.*

After Coventry the Germans bombed other major cities.

'I did my nurse's training in Birmingham between 1939 and 1942. In 1940 the Blitz started. Sleep became scarce. It seemed to become routine: a raid on Tuesday and another on Thursday. We had beds lining the corridors, and shadow hospitals in the basement of Lewis's Store and Ansell's Brewery.' (Joan Nock, Birmingham.)

Southampton was badly bombed in early December. Seventy-four water mains were broken, so the High

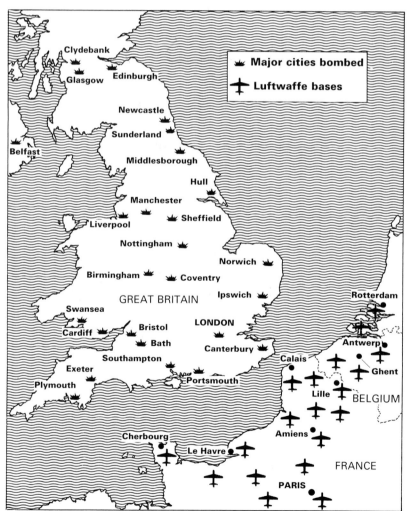

Right *This map shows the major British cities that were German targets during the Blitz.*

Street burned in a whirlwind of fire. The telephone exchange was destroyed. The fires were still burning two days later.

'People who have lived here all their lives don't know the way outside their own doorstep. I've never seen a place so beat – there's not a thing working.' (Mass-Observation Archive.)

The bombing went on: Bristol, Plymouth, Portsmouth, Hull, Clydebank, Sheffield, Manchester, Liverpool, Newcastle upon Tyne and Belfast were among the sixteen cities bombed in the Blitz. Everywhere people had the same sort of experiences.

As the Blitz went on, a new sort of shelter was introduced. It was called a Morrison shelter and was like a big metal dining-table. It was very effective.

'The air raid warden ran along the street shouting "Get in your shelters!" My sister crawled in beside me. My mother was still scrambling in when I saw the walls of the room crumbling and tumbling towards us . . . I cannot remember any sound that night, just the sights – the tumbling walls, the dust and then – I could scarce believe it – the night sky! Our house had completely vanished!' (Gerald Cole, London.)

*People found many different uses for their Morrison shelters! Wire mesh fitted along the sides of the metal table to protect you from flying glass and bricks when you were sheltering underneath.*

# The Fire of London

People got very tired of being woken up every night by the sound of bombs and sirens. Some went to public shelters, or Anderson shelters in the garden. But according to a survey in London in November 1940, 60 per cent of people did not shelter. In a raid they either stayed in bed or dived under the dining-room table.

Fire bombs were causing more and more destruction. In early December, 3,000 fire bombs rained down on London in one night. Then, on 29 December came the worst night in London for fire. It was a Sunday night, so all the City's offices were locked and deserted. The River Thames was at its lowest ebb, and there were no emergency tanks of water.

The German bombers came droning in, following the curving snake of the river. The fire bombs fell in bunches and started fires in empty buildings. Small fires that

*St. Paul's Cathedral, seen above the smoke during the night of 29 December 1940.*

could have been put out by someone on the spot grew into vast blazes. Firemen could not get into locked buildings until it was too late. Soon the City of London was ablaze.

> 'Water had to be relayed from anywhere you could get it (the water mains were broken in the first hour) . . . and pumped through hose lines. And all the time you were bringing up the water, the fire was moving on and moving on.' (Cyril Demarne, London.)

It crept up Ludgate Hill towards St. Paul's Cathedral. The great church stood amid a sea of fire.

> 'It floated but at times it was engulfed and we thought it had gone; then the fiery tide lowered and the Cathedral was above the city as ever.' (H.M. Tomlinson, London, from *A People's War*.)

After this night the government made fire-watching compulsory.

Above left *A poster urging people to start fire-watching. The fires were so bad in London on 29 December that they were close to being fire storms – which is when fires are so strong that people can be sucked into them.*

Above right *Miraculously, St. Paul's Cathedral survived undamaged, although all around was bombed.*

# Fires and Devastation

Fire was the horror of all bombed cities. All along the River Thames in London were docks and warehouses. When the sugar stores at Clydebank were bombed, burning sugar made gluey, fiery rivers which crept from the warehouses like lava from a volcano. Afterwards, when it had cooled, as much as possible was scooped up, to be melted down, cleaned up and used. Food was in short supply in the war!

The Surrey Commercial Docks stored huge supplies of timber. The bombing of Surrey Docks caused an immense fire. Hundreds of firemen came from as far afield as Bristol and Rugby. The fire was an unbroken wall for five kilometres and fireboats on the other side of the river had their paint scorched.

*Firemen at work in London.*

*Cologne, in Germany, was heavily bombed by the Allies.*

*The front page of the* Evening Standard, *14 February 1945. Dresden was devastated by Allied bombing.*

All these fires were obvious from high in the sky: 'When we approached the target at half past two we stared silently into a sea of flames such as none of us had seen before. In Belfast there was not a large number of fires but just one enormous fire.' (German radio reporter on the *Luftwaffe* bombing of Belfast 4–5 May 1941, from *In Time of War*, Robert Fisk.)

By 1943 Britain and the USA were bombing Germany heavily. City after city suffered devastation, death and fire. On 13–14 February 1945 they bombed Dresden:

'At 1.22 a.m. the next wave of planes arrived over the city and dropped approximately 5,000 high explosives and 200,000 incendiaries. This second wave guided by the blaze had only to drop its load into the dark spots to complete the destruction. Their bombs fell into the crowds that had escaped from the already flaming parts of town. Collapsing buildings barred the streets and cut off their escape. Tens of thousands burned to death or suffocated.' (*Overture on the Vistula*.)

# The Last Months of War

The Blitz in Britain finally ended in May 1941. Germany turned its attention to fighting the USSR. Germany's losses in the air raids were far greater than Britain's. As the war dragged on, both sides had given up just bombing factories and docks and deliberately bombed civilian targets.

They had bombed beautiful old cities, killing many innocent people. However, despite all the death and destruction, bombing had not made people want to surrender.

Both sides lost many pilots and crews during bombing raids. Late in the war, Germany began to develop pilotless planes and bombs. The V-1 was first launched

Below right *The German V-1, or 'flying bomb', was a pilotless aeroplane loaded with explosives. When it ran out of fuel it fell out of the sky and blew up on hitting the ground.*

Bottom *There was no effective defence against the V-2. It was much larger and carried far more explosives than the V-1.*

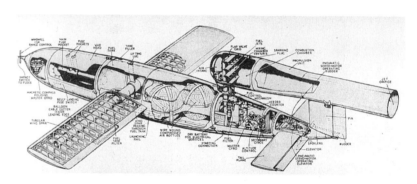

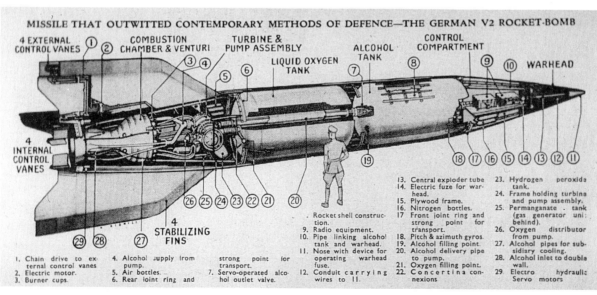

MISSILE THAT OUTWITTED CONTEMPORARY METHODS OF DEFENCE—THE GERMAN V2 ROCKET-BOMB

4 EXTERNAL CONTROL VANES · COMBUSTION CHAMBER & VENTURI · TURBINE & PUMP ASSEMBLY · LIQUID OXYGEN TANK · ALCOHOL TANK · CONTROL COMPARTMENT · WARHEAD · 4 INTERNAL CONTROL VANES · 4 STABILIZING FINS

1. Chain drive to external control vanes.
2. Electric motor.
3. Burner cups.
4. Alcohol supply from pump.
5. Air bottles.
6. Rear joint ring and strong point for transport.
7. Servo-operated alcohol outlet valve.
8. Rocket shell construction.
9. Radio equipment.
10. Pipe linking alcohol tank and warhead.
11. Nose with device for operating warhead fuse.
12. Conduit carrying wires to 11.
13. Central exploder tube.
14. Electric fuze for warhead.
15. Plywood frame.
16. Nitrogen bottles.
17. Front joint ring and strong point for transport.
18. Pitch & azimuth gyros.
19. Alcohol filling point.
20. Alcohol delivery pipe to pump.
21. Oxygen filling point.
22. Concertina connexions.
23. Hydrogen peroxide tank.
24. Frame holding turbine and pump assembly.
25. Permanganate tank (gas generator unit behind).
26. Oxygen distributor from pump.
27. Alcohol pipes for subsidiary cooling.
28. Alcohol inlet to double wall.
29. Electro hydraulic servo motors.

on Britain in June 1944. It was a pilotless plane with an explosive on board.

'We called it the doodlebug or buzzbomb. It was all right as long as you heard the engine. When it went quiet, you knew it had run out of fuel and was coming down.' (J. Walsh, Essex.)

The V-2 was launched three months later. This was an actual rocket, and the first you knew of it was when it exploded.

The British and Americans invaded German-held France in June 1944. By spring 1945 they were capturing the launch pads of the V-1s in northern France. Although V-1s could be shot down by anti-aircraft guns, or attacked by planes, there was no defence against the silent V-2s. The only way they could be stopped was to bomb or capture the launch sites.

Soon the British and Americans were advancing on Germany from one side and the Russians from the other. In May 1945 the war was over in Europe. In August it was over in Japan too.

*By the end of the war much of Germany was badly damaged. This scene in Nuremburg shows how large areas of the city were destroyed.*

# GLOSSARY

**Air Raid Precautions** Things people did to protect themselves from air raids.

**Anderson shelter** An outdoor air raid shelter made from corrugated steel.

**Anti-aircraft guns** Guns for firing at enemy aeroplanes.

**Black-out** Making sure that no lights showed from houses, streets and so on, so that at night towns were invisible from the air.

**CD Respirator** Civilian Duty gas mask.

**Civil Defence** Defending your town or country, even if you are not a soldier.

**Demolished** Knocked down and destroyed.

**Doodlebug** Another name for the V-1. It was also known as the buzzbomb, or robot.

**Incendiary bombs** Small bombs, about half a metre long, that started fires when they exploded.

**Inflatable** Something that can be filled up with air or gas, like a balloon.

**Morrison shelter** An air raid shelter for use indoors, made of a steel table top with wire around it.

**Operation Sealion** Germany's plan to invade Britain.

**Shrapnel** Pieces of metal from shells and bullets.

**Tactics** Plans for how to fight a battle.

**Tarpaulin** Canvas covers, like tents.

**UXB** Unexploded bomb.

# PROJECTS

1 Ask your relations and neighbours if they have any memories of the Blitz. Questions you could ask are: where did you live? What sort of shelter did you use? What did you do in the shelter to pass the time? What sounds do you remember? What was it like after a raid?

2 Imagine you are living at the beginning of the Second World War. What precautions would you take against bombing raids? Think about where you live. What would be the safest part of your home to shelter in?

3 Places to visit:
The Imperial War Museum, London (tel. 01 735 8922)
Eden Camp, Malton, North Yorkshire (A theme museum about civilian life during the Second World War.) (tel. 0653 697777)

# BOOKS TO READ

## Books for younger readers

Nance Lui Fyson, *Growing up in the Second World War* (Batsford, 1981)

Kathleen Monham, *Growing up in World War II* (Wayland, 1979)

Stewart Ross, *How They Lived – A Family in World War II* (Wayland, 1985)

Miriam Moss, *How They Lived – A Schoolchild in World War II* (Wayland, 1988)

Madeline Jones, *Life in Britain in World War II* (Batsford, 1981)

Fiona Reynoldson, *War at Home* (Heinemann Educ., 1980)

Fiona Reynoldson, *War in Europe* (Heinemann Educ., 1980)

## Books for older readers

Peter Chrisp, *The Blitz* (Mass-Observation Archive, University of Sussex Library, 1987)

Robert Westall, *Children of the Blitz* (Penguin, 1985)

## ACKNOWLEDGEMENTS

The publishers would like to thank the following for permitting us to quote from their sources. (The order of sources is as they appear in the text.) Penguin Books Ltd. for *Children of the Blitz* by Robert Westall, 1985. Thames Television for *A People's War* by Peter Lewis, 1986. Extracts from Mass-Observation, copyright the Trustees of the Tom Harrisson Mass-Observation Archive, reproduced by permission of Curtis Brown Group Ltd. Peter Way and Marshall Cavendish for *Shelter People – The War Papers part 12*, 1976. Andre Deutsch Ltd for *In Time of War* by Robert Fisk, 1985. Where sources have a name and location only, they were interviewed by the author.

The illustrations in this book were supplied by the following: E T Archives Limited 29; The Hulton Picture Library *cover;* Imperial War Museum 7 (bottom), 8, 14 (both), 15, 16, 18 (both), 19, 20 (below), 22, 23, 26, 27 (top); John Frost 27 (bottom); Peter Newark's Historical and Military Pictures 4, 5, 9 (both), 11 (bottom), 12, 17 (both), 25 (left), 28 (both); Topham Picture Library 7 (top), 10, 11 (top), 13 (bottom), 20 (inset), 21, 24, 25 (right). The artwork on pages 4 and 22 was supplied by Peter Bull Art Studio.

# INDEX

Air Raid Precautions 6–7,
   **7**, 30
air raid shelters 7
   Anderson shelters **7**,
      14, **19**, 30
   Morrison shelters 23,
      **23**, 30
   public shelters 18–19, **18**
   Underground stations
      14–15, **14**
Air raid wardens 7, 8, 19
air raid warnings 18
Anderson shelters **7**, 14,
   **19**, 30
anti-aircraft guns 12, **13**,
   30

barrage balloons 12
Battle of Britain 5
Black Saturday 12
black-out 8–9, 30
bombing 16–19
   Air Raid Precautions 6–7,
      **7**
   Coventry 20–21, **20**
   other major cities 22–3
   protection against 7
bombs
   doodlebug 29, 30
   fire bombs 24, **25**
   V-1s 28–9

Churchill, Winston **17,
   21**
Civil Defence 7, 30
Coventry, raid on 20–21,
   **20**

damage **12**, 16–17, **16**,
   20–25, **25, 29**
daylight raids 10, 16
doodlebugs 29, 30
Dornier D017 **11**
Dunkirk, retreat from 4

France
   defeated by Germany 4
   liberated from Germany
      29
fire **10**, 11, **11**, 24–7, **26**
firefighting **21**

gas masks 6–7, **6**
Germany 28–9
   bombed by RAF 17, **17**,
      27, **27, 29**
   bombing policy 28–9
   occupation of France 4
   plans to invade Britain
      4–5, 20
   V-1 and V-2 28–9

Hitler, Adolf 4, **4**, 16

invasion of Britain 4–5,
   10, 20

London
   Air Raid Precautions 6
   Blitz 10–28
   damage 16–17, **16**, 20–5
   daylight bombing raids
      10, 16
   fires 11, 24–5
   Underground stations
      14–15, **14**

Morrison shelters 23, **23**,
   30

Operation Sealion 4, **4**

Royal Air Force 5, 17

Salvation Army 15
searchlights 12, **13**
stukas **4**

Underground shelters
   14–15, **14**

V-1 and V-2 28–9, **28**

Wardens 7, 8, 19
Women's Voluntary
   Service 15